Building a World Culture

by

Chris Fife

© 9/16/2017

Table of Contents

Introduction

This book is not intended to propose one world country or a new order in the world. It is not a nationalistic book that has an agency of pushing one nations ideals on another. This book is intended to give ideas about how all nations and people can work together to bring about prosperity and happiness to the world. It is about changing the way we think about the world and about how we work together to face some of the major challenges in the world.

The world has come a long way since Marco Polo brought items from the East to the West and explorers started to connect all of the lands together. The world has become a lot smaller with Columbus and Europe taking possession of the Americas and imposing their beliefs on the native peoples.

The Columbian exchange has brought about a world economy where items are shipped from one country to the next, manufactured, and sold to people around the world. It create a new economic theory of abundance and growth.

Since the British Empire and the spread of values, ideas, and goods around the world the world has truly become a smaller one. Technology has made it so we can travel anywhere in a matter of days not months, and communicate with people in seconds not days. Money can be exchanged instantly and products shipped in days to our front door.

We live in a global society, but we still have a long way to go before we truly are a global society where people can travel in safety, experience the richness of all cultures, and sit down as friends with each other.

Chapter One: Language

In the past when one culture encountered another culture there was a lot of misunderstandings and distrust because of the language barrier. The spread of empires and the extension of a culture brought people together. The Greeks and Romans spread their language to many parts of Europe. Then at one point it was French that was spoken by all of the governments in Europe include Russia where Alexander the Great tried to bring Russia closer to the rest of the countries of Europe.

A common tongue or language is essential for people to communicate with each other. This does not mean that everyone has to speak one language. People throughout the world learn to speak several languages. Throughout Europe people speak their native language and English. This is very useful for many people, because they can speak with family and friends with their native language and for business and governmental affairs they speak English.

Throughout Europe it is difficult for people to make a living especially in tourism if they do not speak English. Many speak several languages in order to communicate with nearby countries. In Switzerland many people speak English, French, and German.

Traveling on a Swiss Airline, the stewardess gave the safety instructions in about five different languages. It was a true example of using language to be able to reach a broader range of people. If it wasn't for this, people would be isolated and lose opportunities. Europe is a good example of communication at its best as people are able to live and work together. This is not the case in other parts of the world.

World Language

Currently English is the world language. The British Empire brought English to Africa, India, China, and many other parts of the world. English is spoken in just about every country in the world and is taught in many schools throughout the world. It has become part of the curriculum in countries like Russia and China.

Since English is the official language of the United States of America with over 300 million people and an economic superpower. People around the world need to speak English in order to do business with the United States. Many people in other countries speak English in order to be able to serve American tourists.

I was surprised at just how well people from France and Switzerland were able to speak English. I have been equally surprised at a couple from Turkey who spoke perfect English and a woman from China who works with my wife. I have also met people from Russia, Africa, and the Middle East who speak good English as well.

In order to join this global community a person needs to be able to speak English and speak it well. It needs to be one of the languages that every child learns in school. It is the language business leaders speak and airplane pilots and air traffic controllers speak.

English is not the easiest language to learn, because it does have a lot of rules and those rules are often broken. It is also a growing language with added vocabulary on a regular basis. It has evolved a lot over the past five hundred years. It has its origins in German. English also has words that have been adopted from French, Spanish, Italian, and Latin.

Many of the new words coming from technology have been added to English and adopted by many other languages like computers and the internet.

Who knows if English will remain the world language. It has endured for over a hundred years. It could very well continue to serve as a dominate language in business and global relations for centuries to come. It is one language that can continue to grow and adapt to the needs of communication for future generations.

Some say Chinese, Urdu, or Spanish may surpass English as the global language. More people do speak Chinese than English, but this is just because China has over a billion people. It doesn't mean a lot of people throughout the world speak it or use it to do business with. This is why English is very important as a world culture. It doesn't mean that everyone should just speak English.

Second Language

There is an argument for a second global language. In order to effectively communicate to people throughout the world they need to be able to speak more than one language. Learning to speak multiple languages also improves communication skills. The brain is able to develop better communication pathways as you learn multiple languages.

We should not have to choose which language should be the second language to learn. It is just a matter of necessity. If you live in Asia or do business in Asia you need to learn Chinese, Japanese, or Urdu. If you are doing business in Latin America you need to know Spanish. If you live in Canada you need to know French. Living in the United States it would be good to be able to know how to speak Spanish, because of the large Spanish speaking population that lives in America.

Children have a disadvantage if they only speak one language. There are many more opportunities for children if they are able to speak multiple languages. Many schools throughout the world offer language programs that help students speak a second language.

Forgotten Languages

Do we then need all of the languages in the world today? One reasonable answer would be no we don't. There are hundreds of local languages that could be forgotten and the world would go on just fine without them. In fact there are a lot of languages over the past hundred years that have become extinct.

There is a problem with this. It hurts local cultures and customs. We do live in a global community and there are only about a dozen languages that everyone speak in the world. Yet there are hundreds of languages that make up the cultures of the world. These unique languages places a special cultural identity for these people. It would be a shame if all of these languages were forgotten.

Gaelic is one of these languages that was almost forgotten. In concerted efforts by many people throughout Scotland they have made Gaelic an official language, it is taught in several schools, and local communities keep it alive. This not only preserves a language it helps to preserve a rich culture in Scotland as well.

The United States in an effort to get rid of American Indian culture send children to boarding schools and forbade them from speaking their native languages. This isolated the children and caused a lot of emotional scares that are still felt in American Indian societies. The efforts of the United States to assimilate the American Indians was a failed experiment, that caused more problems than successes.

It would be wrong to force people to give up speaking their native languages. They should be encouraged to continue to speak their native languages in order to keep their cultural identity. Local communities need to set up ways to preserve their language and their cultural identity to enrich their neighborhoods. The world would be a very different place if none of the local languages were preserved.

Chapter Two: Money

Money is extremely important for a global community. In order to be able to travel to other places or do business with other countries there needs to be a system of using money. In Europe the European Community came up with the idea of a common currency the Euro Dollar. This allows countries that belong to the EU to be able to use Euro dollars instead of having to exchange money all of the time.

Despite the EU's efforts there has been several countries that have been in an economic crisis and the UK never adopted the Euro fully and has since decided to leave the EU. The world's economy is a very complex machine with the United States dollar as a standard. The global economy is intertwined and if something happens to one country it sends a domino effect on the rest of the global economy. Even smaller countries will cause a ripple effect to the larger ones.

World Trade

The first thing that has to happen is that all trade barriers and taxes need to be removed. This enables free enterprise and global competition. The global competition will bring down the prices of goods and encourage companies to become better in order to complete in a global economy. The removal of trade barriers will also help countries to allow more imports and exports to other countries. The consumer base for businesses will increase and everyone will benefit.

Modern technology has made it possible for businesses including small home based businesses to be able to sell and ship to anyone in the world. With the breakdown of barriers countries will be able to bring in more money into their country which will increase the infrastructure, This will help countries to provide more programs for their citizens. Global trade is good for everyone.

Online Shopping

Think about how people in South Dakota could buy homemade jewelry, clothing, furniture, and tourist gifts from Peru, Tibet, or Australia. This is becoming more of a reality than you can believe. Companies like online giant Amazon is able to provide products from all around the world and ship those items to your home in a very short period of time.

Online shopping has been narrowing the gap between countries. The more people buy things on the internet the more there is a need for a global economy. Just think there are no boarders when you buy online. You do not think about the ships, the planes, or the trucks that bring the packages to your door. You just enjoy being able to order something online and then forget about it until it shows up and you can enjoy it.

Credit Cards

In the past people would bring something to trade with another person for the item they wanted. Then there came precious metals that were used such as gold and silver. Then coins and paper money or legal tender which was given to the people from banks who held the gold or silver as collateral for the money they issued. Even the United States and several countries held gold and silver in reserve.

No our money is no backed up with gold or silver. There is still a lot of gold in Fort Knox, but the country is in a lot of debt and the gold would never cover all of the money. This also goes for several countries that are spending more money than they can backup. The deficit spending is based on the potential for money that the country has and the interest the country can pay other countries for their debt. In other words the United States is living off of credit based on the interest it can pay for the debt.

People learned that they could end up going into debt as well. At first this was done strictly through loans, now it can be done with credit cards. People has billions of dollars they owe in credit card bills. It can be a serious issue for many people who owe a lot of money.

Credit cards are not all that bad. In fact the concept of a credit card allows people to be able to buy products online and to buy things just about anywhere without having to carry around a large amount of money or checks. Credit cards enable us to be able to buy things in other countries and automatically exchange the money for us. This is a wonderful thing when you can travel all around the world and just have to bring a small credit card.

You do not even have to bring a credit card with you anymore. You can use an app from your phone to buy items. The technology is such that you can just bring your phone wherever you go and use it to purchase items and use it to get money. The credit card system has brought the world closer to our fingertips. It has brought about a global culture that could very well be the answer to peace and prosperity for the world population.

In order to be able to have a global economy we need to have access to money wherever we go in the world. People should be able to buy money anywhere and businesses should be able to make a living anywhere in the world and have customers from around the world.

There is challenges with this global economy like the sweat shops and slave labor that works in them. People are asked to work in terrible conditions, get paid little, and have little benefits so the company can make a lot more money. The countries of the world need to band together to be able to support businesses and at the same time demand better conditions for their workers by passing regulations especially for foreign companies who pray on their employees naive sense of work.

Chapter Three: Environment

There are some countries in the ocean that may disappear in the coming decades as the Earth warms and the oceans rise. Major cities will go under the ocean and millions of people will be homeless. This is a very serious issue that needs the global community's attention and help. There is no denying it that we are going through climate change and it will drastically impact several countries of the world.

The sad crime of it is that many of these countries effected the most contribute very little to their carbon footprint, and the countries with the largest footprint are doing the least to help prevent this crisis from taking place. Global warming impacts all of us. Pollution does not recognize boarders. Natural disasters do not recognize boarders.

The global community needs to work together to solve environmental concerns. It also needs to be able to address the environmental challenges that come up. Countries need to give add to those who need it. They need to create laws to enforce appliance to environmental standards that will help reverse the process of climate change.

Summits and Treaties

There have been several summits involving countries around the world to discuss solutions to the climate change challenge. There have also been agreements made between countries to be able to control the amount of CO2 put into the atmosphere by countries. Countries have agreed to start reducing their carbon footprint and to make regulations that will work on global climate change.

There problem is that administrations change and laws are not enforced. In other words the summits and treaties become empty promises made to look good in the eyes of the global community. There needs to be some teeth behind the agreements and penalties given to countries that are unable to resolve their own environmental issues. This may anger countries, but it the long run is better off.

Disputes over Issues

Soon if things do not change. Countries will fight each other out of desperation. We have seen this with the refugee crisis coming from Syria. Just think what will happen if there is a global crisis where millions are fleeing their homelands from serious flooding and natural disasters. Think of what will happen when people will no longer be able to live in their countries, will other countries take them in, or will they have to fight in order to survive.

The makeup of the global culture will drastically change if you have entire countries moving into other countries. Countries like North Korea and Iran may take advantage of the situation and attack countries in order to gain power over them. While some countries are dealing with refugees and just trying to survive the climate change other countries will be trying to gain as much power in the world as they can.

Global Environmental Protection

There needs to be a global agency within the United Nations or some other global organization that is in charge of protecting the environment. This could take the form of an environmental police agency that enforces sanctions on countries that are not protecting the environment.

Countries need to start taking responsibility for what they are doing to the environment or their neighbors will become very angry about it. You would not want to live down river from a factory that is polluting the river. Rivers, mountains, lakes, oceans, and forests do not know political boundaries. Nature simply exists where it is and it is the human race that has placed boundaries on it.

If the people of the world are to come together as a global culture we need to be in agreement on how we take care of the environment. All of the countries around the world need to work together to solve the environmental issues we face. This needs to start with the countries that have the biggest carbon footprint the United States and China.

Chapter Four: Human Rights

Human rights has always been an issue since the beginning of time. But these rights were not well defined nor were they guaranteed as dictators, war lords, and kings gained power and subjected the people to slavery and harsh conditions. Today the rights are better defined and guaranteed by many countries through constitutions and the United Nations Declaration on Human Rights which Eleanor Roosevelt helped to bring about.

There are many countries today where there is still human rights violations happening. Dictators, kings, and war lords are still out there hurting their people as they try to have absolute power over their people. It is difficult to be able to get to all of the people of the world to guarantee their safety. In many parts of the world their are gangs and drug cartels that are taking away human rights to the people that live in these areas.

History

In 1754 BC the Code of Hammurabi a Babylonian code of law gave some basic laws governing some rights of the people. It covered items like divorce, liability, slander, and trade. The Greeks came up with democracy where people had a say in the government and the making of laws. The Romans adopted this form of government. Then democracy was abandoned by men who wanted power over the people. In the dark ages kings and lords rule over the people.

In 1215 CE King John of England gave up some of his power to the lords and nobles of England. This allowed for more power to be given to the people. It also paved the way for parliament. But it wasn't until people started to share their ideas with others in an enlightened period of time that human rights became an issue.

The invention of the printing press allowed books and pamphlets to be printed and published to the world. Montesquieu from France spoke of a government that supported the rights of the people. John Locke spoke of the rights of life, liberty, and property. Thomas Paine wrote a book the Rights of Man.

It wasn't until Thomas Jefferson wrote the Declaration of Independence and the famous words, "Inalienable rights… and life, liberty, and the pursuit of happiness…" that the world stood up and took notice. The Declaration of Independence established the United States as a sovereign country, and also declared that everyone was born with universal rights and those rights are life, liberty, and happiness.

The Declaration of Independence set in motion something that brought about human rights for millions of people for many generations. It did not immediately happen nor was it given to all people. Jefferson himself owned slaves and so did many of the founding fathers of the United States. Women were also not given their rights. American Indians were still considered savages and not given the rights of being citizens of the United States. It took several wars and nearly two hundred years to achieve, but the people in America finally have human rights established.

After the revolutionary war the United States was held together by a weak Articles of Confederation that was soon thrown out for the constitution. The American constitution was written through compromise and did not have a bill of rights. Many states already had bill of rights on their state constitutions. There were some who refused to sign the constitution because it did not have a bill of rights. It was not until later that they added a bill of rights which is the first ten amendments to the constitution.

The Bill of Rights guarantees the right to religious freedom, speech, and many other liberties. Many more amendments were added later that added to the rights of the people including the vote for all men, and the vote for women. The political freedom given to the people to vote for representatives and have a say in what laws are made is one of the greatest of the human rights. It allows people to be able to have a say in how things are ran in their country.

Universal Declaration of Human Rights

In 1948 the Universal Declaration of Human Rights was adopted by the United Nations and signed by the United States. It declared many of the rights stated in the amendments of the United States Constitution. The importance of this document is that it is the first document that is a global document on human rights.

It is a document that can be followed by all countries in the world and should be upheld by the countries of the world. When a country does not follow the document they are in violation of human rights and should be held accountable for it. This means that a dictator that hurts his people should be put on trial by the countries of the world for crimes against humanity.

No country or person should be exempt from its message and no person should be allowed to violate the spirit the document is intended to carry out.

The wonderful aspect of the document is that it speaks of everyone in the world regardless of age, sex, nationality, or race. It addresses the serious matters of abuse given to the people of the world.

The declaration covers several different rights and is truly a universal declaration with the intent to address the rights of everyone on the planet. Unfortunately people from many parts of the world are being denied these basic human rights. It is the obligation of the members of the UN as well as other countries of the world to enforce these rights that are spoken of in the declaration of human rights. No one can deny that these rights should be given to everyone.

Life

The right to life is one that could have several different interpretations. This could mean we should not have allow abortions, it could also mean we should not have executions. The right to life in a general sense is that everyone has the right to be able to live without the fear of untimely death or torture. It means that people can live wherever they want without having to be discriminated or abused in any form.

The right to life is that everyone is born equal and dies equal. Children have the right to be able to grow up and live a normal life without abuse or neglect. Women have the right to live as equals to men. People from other countries have the right to live along side people from other countries in harmony.

Everyone has the right to live take a path they choose in life. We have the right to be able to marry, have children, and raise a family without the threat of war or violence. We have the right to live with friends in a mutual bond of fellowship.

Liberty

Freedom often comes at a cost. It is something that should be given to everyone unless a person takes away the freedom of others. We live in a world where children are sold into slave labor, girls are sold into a life of prostitution, and boys are forced to become soldiers. We live in a world where people are slaves to debt, addiction, and oppressive governments.

Children should be free to be children and free from the fear of being kidnapped. Children have the right to be free from bullying and hate. They have the right to be free from parents who abuse them. Children should have the right to an education and be able to have a choice of career they go into.

People have the right to be free from slave labor. People have labor rights to breaks, lunch, and benefits that will help to support them and their families. Everyone have the right to be free from working in an unsafe or abusive environment.

The world needs to be free from addictive substances, pornography, and gambling. People need to be able to be free from being a slave to a mind altering drug, or any drug that forces people to give up everything so they can have on more fix. Children, and women should have the rights to be free from exploitation and pornography. People around the world need to be free from the trap of gambling and the addiction for winning only to lose everything.

People need to be free from the bonds of being in debt. There needs to be a different form of credit and monetary gain that doesn't allow people to get so far in debt that they end up losing everything and then others suffer from them not being able to pay what they owe. It is a terrible thing for people to go into debt without the ability to pay it off. Everyone suffers when debts go unpaid.

Right to Worship

The world is filled with conflicts where Muslim is fighting Christian, Jew is fighting Muslim, and people from other religions are fighting each other. There is a great mistrust, ignorance, and intolerance when it comes to religion. We are still in the dark ages fighting our own crusades. You would think that we would have learned from our mistakes and came up with a plan to work together.

Many parts of the world have come together in harmony with each other. The small island country Mauritius is near the country of Madagascar. It does not have a lot of people and virtually no resources. It did have a turbulent past, but now it is home to people from many different religions, Christians, Hindus, Muslims, and Buddhists. There is virtually no violence, and the people live in harmony with each other.

Many small areas of the world also share this same harmony where people from many different religions live together in peace. It is just a matter of education and tolerance for other beliefs. It is okay to be able to have a neighbor or friend who believes differently than you do.

One of the challenges is how people perceive different religions. There are the stereotypes and a persons own perceptions based on false reports. People may also come to their own conclusions about a religion based on fears from what they see on media reports. When a person hears a report about an extremist group they do not understand the extremist part, only the religion part of it.

Honestly there are good and bad people in all religions. It is not the religion that makes the person evil, it is a combination of many different factors. Many brutal killers were Christian, Jewish, Muslim, and so on. No one can make a blanket statement about a particular religion unless that religion does have in its doctrine or beliefs to harm or hurt innocent people or to damage or take over government. Then it is the responsibility of all of the people to do something about it.

People throughout the world have the right to their own religious beliefs and thoughts. They have the right to worship in a manner pleasing to them. Religion often gives people hope and solitude, threaten their very faith and they will fight back. It is not a good thing for religious wars to be going on around the world. It is also not a good thing to restrict or kick out people because they belong to a certain religion. This is something we need to overcome and put this awful practice in the past.

Right to Free Speech

Freedom of the press and freedom to share your ideas with others benefits the world. This is what brought about the technology we have today, the enlightened governments of the world, and more freedom than any other time in history. It all started with the printing press and the spreading of the word and ideas to people around the world.

Today people can text or post things on the internet for people to see throughout the world. It was this freedom to express ideas that led to many people overthrowing corrupt governments. It was also the corrupt government that tried to stop the freedom of speech. This is becoming hard to do as people have access to more technology. It is only those who are not able to read or listen to what is happening in the world that or isolated and have lost their freedoms.

Places like North Korea, remote places, or destitute places where people are denied freedoms of speech and the ability to communicate with the world and learn what other people are doing. Women living in countries where they are oppressed are getting information that many other parts of the world women have equality and human rights. Children are learning about just what types of opportunities there are outside of their countries.

Interpretation of Rights

A universal set of rights for everyone can be a hard thing to do. Despite the Declaration of Independence, and the Constitution of the United States there have been people who have been abused throughout history in the United States. It has taken other amendments to the constitution and the Supreme Court to interpret the laws of the land to determine if they were constitutional or if people's rights were being violated.

The interpretation of those right has led to a lot of debate over the years. This has brought about debates over abortion, women's rights, gay and lesbian rights, and many other issues that could have several different meanings. The rights could even change over time to fit the time period in which the rights are being evaluated.

The right to bare arms is one such right that has been hotly debated. Do we really need guns today? Some people would argue we need guns more than ever, others would say we don't need guns.

One person's right may interfere with another person's right. When this happens these rights need to be evaluated. A person doesn't have the right to say false things about another person, verbally abuse the person, or be mean to others and do it under freedom of speech. A person cannot play loud music all night long keeping other people awake.

It is just like how children have the right to an education, but if a child does something to interfere with the education of other children the child needs to be removed from the classroom so other children can learn. This could mean that a student who wears a shirt that has vulgar language on it needs to be removed from the school, because it causes too much of a distraction for other students to be able to learn in class.

A business owner may remove a customer from their business if the customer poses a threat to other people at the business or interfere with the business from serving its customers. If this was not so, many businesses would go out of business. Now how the business goes about treating their customers or removing their customers is another story.

Chapter Five: Security

The United States is often referred to as the police of the world. When I went in and talked with a Marine recruiter he mentioned that it was the Marines who often went in first to deal with global issues. Why is the United States going in to handle other countries problems? Why do we need global police?

The United Nations is suppose to be able to send in peace keepers who act as police, but they are often given limited power and are subject to the countries they are sent to. The United States often sends the bulk of the military in global crosses, because the United States has the greatest military resources of any country in the world, and a safe peaceful world is a very good think in terms of the economy and in foreign relations.

In order to have a world culture their needs to be security from violence, oppression, and tyranny. We cannot have economic freedom and prosperity if there is a threat of war. Human rights violations become rampant when countries are having civil wars. All communications break down when there are conflicts.

Internal Conflicts

It can be difficult to maintain the peace in the world when there are so many internal conflicts. Every country in the world deals with internal conflicts of domestic violence, gang warfare, and criminal behavior. There are several countries of the world that are so involved in trying to solve their own problems they are not in the position to help other countries when a conflict arises. This is why it is important to countries to help each other solve the challenges of internal conflicts.

There needs to be international cooperation in combating many of the social ills that create the problems. Drug use and distribution is one such problems that needs to have international cooperation in order to resolve the problem. This includes dealing with drug cartels and drug lords that invoke terror in local communities.

Many neighboring countries have to work together in order to stop the spread of violence and the spillover of war into other countries. Syria is such an example where a civil war has resulted in multiple rebel and terrorist groups rising to power and the problems in Syria spilling over into the neighboring countries of Lebanon, Jordan, Turkey, and Iraq.

The crisis in Syria has continued to get worse. Several countries including Syria's neighbors have helped refugees. Yet there has been little that has been resolved in the country. Many larger countries like Saudi Arabia and Iran are supporting different rebel groups. The United States and Russia are also supporting different groups in an effort to put into power a faction they like. This just makes for a very dangerous chess game between superpowers.

Genocide

There have been many horrible genocides that have taken place throughout history in many different forms. In the Americas the native peoples were nearly wiped out from disease, starvation, and war. The Jewish people have been targets of genocide throughout history. The Armenians during World War I in Turkey were targeted to be killed and driven from the country. There was the killing fields of Cambodia and Rwanda and Sudan. In Europe there was Bosnia.

Genocide is still a threat around the world. There is an important need for a world security force that can act in a minutes notice to respond to acts of genocide around the world in order to protect innocent people and to prevent further atrocities. Many of the recent genocides that has taken place could have been prevented or at least stopped before it cost a lot of lives with the help of an international security force.

The United Nation peace keeping troops that have gone into different areas of the world is a start, but it is often not given the authority to engage the enemy or be a powerful enough presence to prevent violence from happening. There were UN troops in Rwanda when the genocide started and they were unable to prevent it. If it wasn't for a Tutsi military invasion that captured the government the genocide would have continued. The French finally came in and set up refugee camps and provided some security in the country.

Rwanda was an example of the failure of the global community to act in a crisis and nearly one million people died as a result. All of this happening in three months. Without the security we need in the world, the fragile peace many countries now have will be gone. This is one reason why the United States has taken charge in stabilizing many areas of the world. Yet even the United States has not helped to prevent many of the problems in the world. The United States was not involved in Rwanda.

The United States has been criticized for its involvement around the world in dealing with crisis situations. Many countries believe that the United States is too aggressive in dealing with other countries. There was a lot of debate over our involvement in Afghanistan and Iraq. Both countries which were being led by oppressive governments that were killing and torturing their own people.

Cooperation

The only way to truly deal with global conflicts is to have the cooperation of all countries in the effort to handle these challenges. If the United States goes into a country to deal with a crisis, it becomes a temporary fix and makes a lot of other countries angry. But if countries work together to resolve the conflicts, and the countries come up with solutions together the conflicts can end up with long lasting results that can benefit the global community.

This happened when Kuwait was invaded by Iraq. The United States sought cooperation from dozens of countries including Kuwait's neighbors in dealing with Iraq. It was an international force with cooperation from several countries. The result was very positive with very little casualties. The only problem was that after the war was over, there was no plan for long term stability in the region with Iraq.

Security inspectors were to go into Iraq to make sure Saddam Hussain wasn't planning anything, but there was no real teeth behind the inspectors and so Saddam Hussain put on a facade and then finally told them they could not come into the country. It was again the United States that took charge to remove Saddam Hussain from power, but this time it was done with little international cooperation and many countries of the world were upset about the US involvement.

Cooperation needs to take place in order to global security to happen. It needs to be swift to act in order to stop further deaths when it comes to global conflicts. If the international community would have worked together swiftly in combating the conflicts World War II would have been prevented.

Crimes against Humanity

The global security force needs to identify crimes against humanity and go after those individuals and try them in court. The security force needs to have the power to remove kings, dictators, and presidents from power if they feel that it is necessary for the welfare of the world and the protection of the people of the country. This could pose as a problem as in the case of Saddam Hussain who does not want to leave quietly.

The security force needs to have enough international cooperation and power to be able to invade a country and remove the leader from power and do it quickly. With enough power the leaders of the world will treat their people with more dignity and respect. We can once and for all get ride of corrupt evil individuals who hurt innocent people. If the people of the world new that they could be held to a higher standard in the world for human rights many of them would think twice before committing crimes against humanity.

This has been done several times starting with the Nazi leaders during World War II who were involved in the Holocaust. Since then there have been few who have been actually tried and convicted like Saddam Hussain. There are still many leaders around the world that could be taken and tried for crimes against humanity and removed from power.

Chapter Six: Tolerance

There cannot be a global culture without tolerance. People cannot work together, live, and play together without some amount of tolerance for the differences in the world. Many of the conflicts throughout the world are because of intolerance. How can people help others if their is no tolerance for others?

Education

First their needs to be a global curriculum that building a foundation of tolerance for the next generation. Part of the problems in the world today is that children are being taught to hate or fear different groups in their homes or even in school. The propaganda that exists in the world needs to end and a focused effort needs to be established in order for the next generation to get rid of their fears, hate, and intolerance towards others.

Many of the century old conflicts could be resolved in one generation if the children were taught tolerance at home and in school. It needs to be a global effort in educating children so they can grow up without the prejudice that is often passed from one generation to the next.

There are some people in the world who will never have tolerance for others and will continue to hold on to their prejudices. But it is the children who can change and will grow up with a different set of beliefs and a different attitude towards other people as well as a sense of tolerance.

How can we teach tolerance in schools? Children can learn about different cultures of the world. By learning about cultures they are able to have a better understanding of what others think and believe, and they will not fear other people as much. It is generally through ignorance that people become intolerant of other people. By also teaching about compassion and kindness towards others it will help them to build tolerance for other cultures.

Children need to understand that tolerance leads to cooperation, friendship, and harmony among others. It will also lead to a better understanding of how the world works and how to become more successful. Becoming tolerant of others allows others to be tolerant of you.

Religion

I could not write a book about world culture without writing about religion. There cannot be a world culture without religion and without religious tolerance. A world culture does not mean there will be one religion. It doesn't mean that we will have a battle where the people of one religion kills those of another religion. This has already been taking place and continues to happen, but it doesn't solve anything. It just means a lot of people are dying for nothing.

Jesus Christ did not say kill your neighbor, the Buddha did not say slay unbelievers, sure there were times when in the sacred texts it talked about killing certain people, but we live in very different times. We live in a time when we can achieve world peace, we can live together in harmony, and we can be tolerant of other religions.

Everyone who is born on the earth no matter where they were born should have the right to choose what they believe and what religion they want to belong to. If a person wants to change religions they have that right. If a person wants to be an atheist the person has that right.

The problem comes when their is religious intolerance and people refuse to allow people to choose and they force them to belong to a religion, or force them to worship a certain way. Religious people around the world should not force their religion on other people and be tolerant of what other people believe. This means that they do not show bias, or discriminate people because they belong to a different religion.

Stereotypes need to be dispelled when it comes to religions. Muslims are not terrorists, Jewish people are not bankers, Mormons do not have more than one wife, and Buddhists do not sit around all day long meditating and chanting. We create intolerance out of fear and ignorance based on stereotypes that are not true.

Lifestyle

Another area a global culture needs to be tolerant of, is people's lifestyle. It does not mean we need to agree with the decisions people make or what lifestyle they choose we just need to treat them with respect and dignity without discrimination. Everyone needs to be able to have a spirit of tolerance and respect for the different lifestyles people choose to follow.

Lifestyles may include such things as; sexual orientation, a persons diet, what a person wears, people who choose to get tattoos, a person's career choice, or where a person chooses to live. It could even be things like what music a person likes to listen to or what sports he likes to watch or play.

Tolerance does not mean acceptance of the lifestyle or having to do what other people are doing. You do not have to listen to music you hate to have tolerance for a person who likes music you hate. Tolerance also comes with responsibility. We do not want to impose our lifestyle on others. Nor do we want them imposing their lifestyle on us.

I teach a lot of children who have a lifestyle that is opposite of mine, and they have parents who live this way as well. Even though we have opposing lifestyles I am still able to befriend these students, teach them, and grade them fairly. Just as long as they do not interfere with the learning of other students, I can tolerate their lifestyle. It is when their lifestyle interfere with the learning of other students, I have to step in and prevent this.

Acceptance

We need to accept people for who they are and not try to force them to change. The experiment of trying to force change on someone has failed miserably several times. It only brings violence and war. It also brings abuse and despair for those who do not want to change. Columbus after landing in the new world set about forcing the native peoples to be slaves. This caused a radical change for the people and within 50 years the entire people was gone. Many of them died from disease, but there were several who ended up committing suicide. Columbus wrote that the people when he first met them were the happiest he had ever seen.

The Aborigines of Australia and the American Indians of North America both were subjects to forced changes. Both groups are still attempting to recover from such changes. They have the highest rate of unemployment in their countries, and suffer from poor health.

It is important to accept people for who they are and to come to common ground a set of common social norms. This is done throughout the world where people from different lifestyles and cultures are able to interact with other people as mutual friends. I see this at national parks where people from all over the world come together to see the wonders of nature.

Think of it, millions of people coming together year after year and getting along with each other without too many serious problems. The only serious problems is the interaction with the wildlife and even then if the people follow the accepted regulations of the park no one gets hurt. It is this acceptance of common regulations that makes things work. Without organization or common regulations there would be some serious consequences.

I believe that the national park example works, because people are coming together to experience something great, something fun, and something they have never seen before. Their is no ill intent when people visit a national park. They are there to have a good time. Such attitude brings about a positive atmosphere. I also noticed many of the employees are from different countries as well. It is as if they are international ambassadors working for the national park service. It is a great model for a world culture.

Chapter Seven: Diversity

A world culture would not be complete without diversity. When it comes to humans it is difficult to put everyone into one general category. People are very different from each other. Even identical twins have their own unique personality. This is one reason why there are so many problems when it is assumed that we can assimilate people into just one identical culture.

The success and failure of the United States of America in building an American culture is an example of how diversity is essential. Many people believed in the past that America had to be a melting pot of cultures in order to come out with an American culture. People has to be assimilated into the culture thus giving up their old culture and accepting the new. This was a failure in terms that when people attempted to give up their old culture they lost their identity.

The attitude of having a melting pot in America brought about racism, bigotry, and intolerance for outside cultures. It also brought about a level of fear for anyone who did not embrace the American culture. Today the United States still struggles with being able to accept the diversity of others. People cannot be treated like numbers.

The success that comes in America does come from the diversity of the cultures in the country. It is this diversity that brings richness and vibrance to the American culture. If it wasn't for this diversity the United States would be a much smaller and weaker country. The regions of the country have their own unique culture and way of doing things, and within each region there are many other cultures. America is known for being the land of opportunity and a land of many different cultures. Just about every country in the world is represented by the people who have come to America, which makes it more of a world culture in itself.

It is an ongoing experiment that has its ups and downs. There tends to be pockets of cultural neighborhoods around where people speak their native language and share the same traditions with their neighborhood friends and relatives. Then venture outside their neighborhood to go to the shopping store, theatre, or to school or work. Then they have to try to belong to another culture with a different language and traditions they have to embrace or be ostracized.

It can be a very difficult situation for most people coming into a different country to be able to fit in. This has been brought to light with the amount of refugees coming from Syria into Europe and around the world. How do refugees coop with moving to another country? How do the countries receiving the refugees handle the demands? In a global culture the process of dealing with refugees would be much more simple.

Benefits of Diversity

There are many benefits of having a diverse population. Scientifically it makes the gene pool stronger and people are able to resist more diseases and tend to healthier. Diversity also brings more ideas and opinions to the table when facing challenges. You probably have heard the saying that two heads are better than one. Having people from many different background is better than having people from the same background. The world would be a far better place if scientists, doctors, politicians, and professionals worked together from all around the world.

We would be able to accomplish so much more if instead of just working with people from a small community, or country we worked with people around the world to solve issues. The peace process would get down quicker and more effectively if everyone was involved instead of just a handful of dignitaries. The diversity of people adds a lot to working out challenges in the world.

The richness of diverse cultures helps to bring spice to life. Imagine eating the same thing every day for the rest of your life. Now imagine being able to each different things from all over the world and having something different every day. Imagine the same thing with music, movies, the clothes you wear, and the places you travel to.

Diversity makes life exciting and fun as people get to know people from other backgrounds and culture. How boring it would be if astronauts went to the stars and found other civilizations in other worlds and they were exactly like ours. Think how boring books or movies would be if they were all the same. You would read one book and then never read again, or watch one movie and then never watch anymore movies.

Melting Pot or Salad

Should the world culture be a melting pot where all of the cultures dissolve into one unified culture and the rest of the cultures disappear? Can a melting pot approach work? Is it healthy to force people to give up their language, traditions, and fundamentals in their culture? This does have some benefits, but too much would be lost in the process.

A world culture should be as diverse as a good salad. If you have a salad with only a couple ingredients in it, the salad is not that good, not a lot of taste, and lacks the nutrition to be healthy. A good salad has several ingredients that adds flavor and increases the nutritional quality of the salad. You might add beans, rice, several types of lettuce, berries, and a dressing to the salad.

People from another culture brings with them experience, music, art, science, technology, and traditions. They can also add to the moral fiber of a community. There is so much diverse cultures can do for a community, especially when the community needs skilled workers and fresh faces to help the community.

In many places in the world with zero or even negative population growth the influx of immigrants is vital to the economy and sustainability of the country. There may be a point in a countries history where the country will be looking for people to come to the country to live so they can have enough workers to fill all of the vacancies that have not been filled. It is the increase of immigrants that help countries to create a balance in their population.

Need for Diversity

There needs to be diversity throughout the world in order to be able to build a strong global culture that will last throughout the ages. It will make the countries of the world stronger, and will push science and technology even further than we have it today. Nothing is better at breaking through plateaus in science and technology than to have a diverse population working of solving some pressing issues.

Many countries that are having problems today are not very diverse. These countries have remained isolated from the rest of the world. Trade suffers when a country is not diverse. Education and domestic situations deteriorate, because there is no diversity. Countries need a diverse population in order to be able to survive the world in which we live.

Chapter Eight: Harmony

There is a lot of effort we need to take, before there is a global culture. Many parts in the world are still divided through bitter enemies and intolerance. There are also remote areas of the world where little is known about the world culture. It will take several more decades to be able to achieve a harmonious world culture. It will take a lot of effort in the global community with cooperation from governments and people. It will take private organizations to bridge the gap between countries and people living in remote regions of the world.

Conflicts

The conflicts of the world need to be resolved with the help of an international community working together to negotiate a peace agreement. The peace needs to resolved in such a way as to have long lasting peace and not just a means to temporary holt the bloodshed. Countries need to work together in order to be able to resolve domestic violence and abuse in the world.

Long lasting resentments and embittered hatreds towards groups needs to end also with the help of an international community. The ongoing conflict in Israel needs to be resolved. The threat from countries like North Korean needs to be resolved. The ongoing instability of third world countries needs to be resolved. All of these conflicts around the world need the help of an international team to finally put an end to the violence.

People who continue to hurt other people need to be arrested and tried for crimes against humanity. Military leaders and leaders of countries who continue the conflicts in their own countries and abroad need to be put on trial for their crimes. The people of the world need to rise up and say, "No more hate and violence"!

Poverty

There needs to be an end of poverty in the world. Countries and private organizations along with the help of all people need to find a way to end the poverty of the world especially those areas of the world that are hit the worst. There is enough abundance of food, shelter, and resources to be able to provide the basics to people. There is also the means to be able to put everyone to work.

The inequality of pay in the world needs to be examined as well. This means there needs to be gender equality with salaries as well as equalizing pay in careers. A teacher, police officer, or nurse should have higher wages while the athlete or actor should be making less. People should be have access to more education in their careers with incentives from their employers.

It is hard to raise people out of poverty if they are stuck in a cycle of generational poverty without the opportunities to get out. This is where people need to have the opportunity for education, training, and assistance. This could also mean people receive medical or mental health care as well. There needs to be a way to break the cycle.

Common Ground

There needs to be common ground in order to have a world culture. It is okay for people of different backgrounds and cultures to be able to live in harmony together, but they also need some common ground. Common ground enables people to be able to work together to solve the most critical issues in life.

A common language is the most important in order for people to be able to communicate with each other. This could be one language like English people can speak together and then they can also continue to speak their native language as well as languages in their local area to be able to communicate with people effectively. People will have to be bilingual knowing at least two languages and in some regions of the world more.

There needs to be a common educational system where children learn a world culture of cooperation and tolerance. Children need to be able to understand the global economy and the career skills in order to be able to be prepared for the future. The world education system will be able to bring cultures around the world together and bring a true sense of harmony and cooperation in science and technology.

The world needs a world economic system where there is free trade and business relationships. A common currency and a system to combat recessions, and the collapse of economic systems around the world. It is hard to have a world culture without a common economic system and be able to resolve many of the other issues in the world.

A world health care system also needs to be in place so that when a natural disaster hits people are ready and don't have to rely on private organizations like the Red Cross to come in and save people. The health care system can also go to places where people desperately need the help and epidemics like the one in Africa of Ebola can be contained quickly. Children will be able to grow up healthier and be able to contribute to society instead of being a burden on society.

Moving Forward

The world is already moving towards a world culture. It is only those who want to hold on to their nationalistic ideas and still have hate towards other people that are preventing a world culture to come together. There is for the most part a common language, there is the United Nations that can take charge in many affairs, there is the World Health Organization (WHO), Europe has made an attempt at the globalization of Europe with the EU, countries continue to seek the aid and cooperation of other countries, and many people want a world culture.

There does need to be some caution and examination of attempts at a world culture. Individual cultures need to be preserved in order to continue to have a diverse world. There needs to be tolerance for religions of the world, different lifestyles, and different points of view. Countries need to cooperate with each other and talk things out before a misunderstanding turns into a war.

World Culture Checklist

- Common Language
- Common Educational System
- Common Health Care
- Common Currency and Economical system (Free Trade)
- International Police Force and court
- Preservation of Individual Cultures
- International Environmental Protection Agency